The United States Constitution

for Know-It-Alls

DISCARD

Filiquarian Publishing, LLC.

Filiquarian Publishing, LLC is publishing this edition of The United States Constitution for Know-It-Alls, due to its status under the GNU Free Documentation License.

The cover of The United States Constitution for Know-It-Alls, and "For Know-It-Alls" imprint is copyright 2008, Filiquarian Publishing, LLC.

The United States Constitution for Know-It-Alls
is available for free download at
www.know-it-alls.com/dbooks/U688

Filiquarian Publishing, LLC.

The United States Constitution
for Know-It-Alls

The United States Constitution is the supreme law of the United States of America. It was adopted on September 17, 1787, by the Constitutional Convention in Philadelphia, Pennsylvania, and later ratified by conventions in each state in the name of "the People"; it has since been amended twenty-seven times.[1][2] The Constitution has a central place in United States law and political culture.[3] The U.S. Constitution is argued by many to be the oldest written national constitution.[4] The handwritten, or "engrossed", original document is on display at the National Archives and Records Administration in Washington, D.C. The United States Constitution has 4,543 words, including the signatures, and takes approximately 30 minutes to read.[5]

History

Drafting and Ratification Requirements

In September 1786, commissioners from five states met in the Annapolis Convention to discuss adjustments to the Articles of Confederation that would improve commerce. They invited state representatives to convene in Philadelphia to discuss improvements to the federal government. After debate, the Congress of the Confederation endorsed the plan to revise the Articles of Confederation on February 21, 1787.[6] Twelve states, Rhode Island being the only exception, accepted this invitation and sent delegates to convene in May 1787.[6] The resolution calling the Convention specified that its purpose was to propose amendments to the Articles, but the Convention decided to propose a rewritten Constitution.[7] The Philadelphia Convention voted to keep the deliberations top secret and decided to draft a new fundamental government design which eventually stipulated that only nine of the thirteen states would have to ratify for the new government to go into effect (for the

4

participating states).[7] Our knowledge of the drafting and construction of the United States Constitution comes primarily from the diaries left by James Madison, who kept a complete record of the proceedings at the Constitutional Convention.[8]

Work of the Philadelphia Convention

The Virginia Plan was the unofficial agenda for the Convention, and was drafted chiefly by James Madison, considered to be "The Father of the Constitution" for his major contributions.[8] It was weighted toward the interests of the larger states, and proposed among other points:

* A powerful bicameral legislature with House and Senate[9]

* An executive chosen by the legislature

* A judiciary, with life-terms of service and vague powers

* The national legislature would be able to veto state laws

An alternative proposal, William Patterson's New Jersey Plan, gave states equal weights and was supported by the smaller states.[10] Roger Sherman of Connecticut brokered The Great Compromise whereby the House would represent population, the Senate would represent states, and a powerful president would be elected by elite electors.[11] Slavery was not explicitly mentioned, but 3/5 of the number of slaves would be counted toward the population used to apportion the House, and runaway slaves would have to be returned.

Ratification

Contrary to the process for "alteration" spelled out in Article 13 of the Articles of Confederation, Congress submitted the proposal to the states and set the terms for representation.

On September 17, 1787, the Constitution was completed in Philadelphia at the Federal Convention, followed by a speech given by Benjamin Franklin who urged unanimity, although they decided they only needed nine states to ratify

the constitution for it to go into effec
Convention submitted the Constitution
Congress of the Confederation, where it received
approval according to Article 13 of the Articles of
Confederation, but the resolution of the Congress
submitting the Constitution to the states for
ratification and agreeing with its provision for
implementation upon ratification by nine states is
contrary to Article 13, though eventually all
thirteen states did ratify the Constitution, albeit
after it took effect.

After fierce fights over ratification in many of the
states, New Hampshire became that ninth state on
June 21, 1788.[9] Once the Congress of the
Confederation received word of New Hampshire's
ratification, it set a timetable for the start of
operations under the Constitution, and on March
4, 1789, the government under the Constitution
began operations.

Historical Influences

Several of the ideas in the Constitution were new,
and a large number of ideas were drawn from the
literature of Republicanism in the United States,

from the experiences of the 13 states, and from the British experience with mixed government. The most important influence from the European continent was from Montesquieu, who emphasized the need to have balanced forces pushing against each other to prevent tyranny. (This in itself reflects the influence of Polybius' 2nd century BC treatise on the checks and balances of the constitution of the Roman Republic.) John Locke is known to have been a major influence, and the due process clause of the United States Constitution was partly based on common law stretching back to the Magna Carta of 1215.[9] Another leading influential force was that of the Iroquois Confederacy which had set a basis for the United States Constitution as well as the Articles of Confederation.

Influences on the Bill of Rights

The United States Bill of Rights were the ten amendments added to the Constitution in 1791, as the supporters had promised opponents during the debates of 1788.[12] The English Bill of Rights (1689) was an inspiration for the American Bill of Rights. For example, both require jury trials, contain a right to bear arms, and prohibit excessive bail as well as "cruel and unusual punishments." Many liberties protected by state constitutions and the Virginia Declaration of Rights were incorporated into the United States Bill of Rights.

Articles of the Constitution

The Constitution consists of a preamble, seven original articles, twenty-seven amendments, and a paragraph certifying its enactment by the constitutional convention.

Preamble: Statement of Purpose

The Preamble states:

"We the People of the United States, in Order to form a more perfect Union, establish Justice, insure domestic Tranquility, provide for the common defence, promote the general Welfare, and secure the Blessings of Liberty to ourselves and our Posterity, do ordain and establish this Constitution for the United States of America."

The Preamble neither grants any powers nor inhibits any actions; it only explains the rationale behind the Constitution and notes by what authority it is enacted. The preamble is a basic statement of purpose that precedes the constitution. The Preamble, especially the first three words ("We the people"), is one of the most-quoted sections of the Constitution.

Article One: Legislative Power

Article One establishes the legislative branch of government, the United States Congress, which includes the House of Representatives and the Senate. The Article establishes the manner of election and qualifications of members of each House. In addition, it provides for free debate in Congress and limits self-serving behavior of congressmen, outlines legislative procedure and indicates the powers of the legislative branch. There is a debate as to whether the powers listed in Article 1 Section 8 are a list of enumerated powers. These powers may also be interpreted as a list of powers, formerly either executive or judicial in nature, that have been explicitly granted to the U.S. Congress. This interpretation may be further supported by a broad definition of both the commerce clause and the necessary-and-proper clause of the Constitution. The argument for enumerated powers can be traced back to the 1819 McCulloch v. Maryland United States Supreme Court ruling. Finally, it establishes limits on federal and state legislative power.

Article Two: Executive Power

Article Two describes the presidency (the executive branch): procedures for the selection of the president, qualifications for office, the oath to be affirmed and the powers and duties of the office. It also provides for the office of Vice President of the United States, and specifies that the Vice President succeeds to the presidency if the President is incapacitated, dies, or resigns, although whether this succession was on an acting or permanent basis was left unclear. In practice, this has always been treated as succession, and the 25th Amendment provides explicitly for succession. Article Two also provides for the impeachment and removal from office of civil officers (the President, Vice President, judges, and others).

Article Three: Judicial Power

Article Three describes the court system (the judicial branch), including the supreme Court. The article requires that there be one court called the supreme Court; Congress, at its discretion, can create lower courts, whose judgments and orders are reviewable by the supreme Court. Article Three also requires trial by jury in all criminal cases, defines the crime of treason, and charges Congress with providing for a punishment for it. It also sets the kinds of cases that may be heard by the federal judiciary, which cases the supreme Court may hear first (called original jurisdiction), and that all other cases heard by the supreme Court are by appeal.

Article Four: States' Powers and Limits

Article Four describes the relationship between the states and the Federal government and amongst the states. For instance, it requires states to give "full faith and credit" to the public acts, records and court proceedings of the other states. Congress is permitted to regulate the manner in which proof of such acts, records or proceedings may be admitted. The "privileges and immunities" clause prohibits state governments from discriminating against citizens of other states in favor of resident citizens (e.g., having tougher penalties for residents of Ohio convicted of crimes within Michigan). It also establishes extradition between the states, as well as laying down a legal basis for freedom of movement and travel amongst the states. Today, this provision is sometimes taken for granted, especially by citizens who live near state borders; but in the days of the Articles of Confederation, crossing state lines was often a much more arduous (and costly) process. Article Four also provides for the creation and admission of new states. The Territorial Clause gives Congress the power to make rules for disposing of Federal property and governing non-state territories of the United States. Finally, the fourth section of Article Four requires the United States to guarantee to each state a republican form of government, and to protect the states from invasion and violence.

Article Five: Process of Amendments

Article Five describes the process necessary to amend the Constitution. It establishes two methods of proposing amendments: by Congress or by a national convention requested by the states. Under the first method, Congress can propose an amendment by a two-thirds vote (of a quorum, not necessarily of the entire body) of the Senate and of the House of Representatives. Under the second method, two-thirds (2/3) of the state legislatures may convene and "apply" to Congress to hold a national convention, whereupon Congress must call such a convention for the purpose of considering amendments. As of 2008, only the first method (proposal by Congress) has been used.

Once proposed—whether submitted by Congress or by a national convention—amendments must then be ratified by three-fourths (3/4) of the states to take effect. Article Five gives Congress the option of requiring ratification by state legislatures or by special conventions assembled in the states. The convention method of ratification has been used only once (to approve the 21st Amendment). Article Five currently places only one limitation on the amending power—that no amendment can deprive a state of its equal representation in the Senate without that state's consent.

Article Six: Federal Power

Article Six establishes the Constitution, and the laws and treaties of the United States made in accordance with it, to be the supreme law of the land, and that "the judges in every state shall be bound thereby, any thing in the laws or constitutions of any state notwithstanding." It also validates national debt created under the Articles of Confederation and requires that all legislators, federal officers, and judges take oaths or affirmations to "support" the Constitution. This means that the states' constitutions and laws should not conflict with the laws of the federal constitution—and that in case of a conflict, state judges are legally bound to honor the federal laws and constitution over those of any state.

Article Six also states "no religious Test shall ever be required as a Qualification to any Office or public Trust under the United States".

Article Seven: Ratification

Article Seven sets forth the requirements for ratification of the Constitution. The Constitution would not take effect until at least nine states had ratified the Constitution in state conventions specially convened for that purpose. (See above Drafting and ratification requirements.)

Provisions for Amendment

The authors of the Constitution were clearly aware that changes would be necessary from time to time if the Constitution was to endure and cope with the effects of the anticipated growth of the nation. However, they were also conscious that such change should not be easy, lest it permit ill-conceived and hastily passed amendments. Balancing this, they also wanted to ensure that an overly rigid requirement of unanimity would not block action desired by the vast majority of the population. Their solution was to devise a dual process by which the Constitution could be altered.

Unlike most constitutions, amendments to the U.S. constitution are appended to the existing body of the text, rather than being revisions of or insertions into the main articles. There is no provision for expunging from the text obsolete or rescinded provisions.

Aside from the direct process of amending the Constitution, the practical effect of its provisions may be altered by judicial decision and review. The United States is a common law country, rooted in English common law, with courts following the precedents established in prior cases. However, when a U.S. Supreme Court decision clarifies the application of a part of the Constitution to existing law, the effect is to establish the meaning of that part for all practical purposes. Not long after adoption of the Constitution, in the 1803 case of Marbury v. Madison the Supreme Court established the doctrine of judicial review, which is the power of the Court to examine legislation and other acts of Congress and to decide their constitutionality. The doctrine also embraces the power of the Court to explain the meaning of various sections of the Constitution as they apply to particular cases brought before the Court. Since such cases will reflect changing legal, political, economic, and social conditions, this provides a mechanism, in practice, for adjusting the Constitution without needing to amend its text. Over the years, a series of Court decisions, on issues ranging from governmental regulation of radio and television to the rights of the accused in criminal cases, has affected a change in the way many Constitutional clauses are interpreted, without amendment to the actual text of the Constitution.

Congressional legislation, passed to implement provisions of the Constitution or to adapt those implementations to changing conditions, also broadens and, in subtle ways, changes the meanings given to the words of the Constitution. Up to a point, the rules and regulations of the many agencies of the federal government have a similar effect. In case of objection, the test in both cases is whether, in the opinion of the courts, such legislation and rules conform with the meanings given to the words of the Constitution.

Amendments

The Constitution has a total of 27 amendments. The first ten, collectively known as the Bill of Rights, were ratified simultaneously. The following seventeen were ratified separately.

The Bill of Rights (1–10)

The Bill of Rights comprises the first ten amendments to the Constitution. Those amendments were adopted between 1789 and 1791, and all relate to limiting the power of the federal government. They were added in response to criticisms of the Constitution by the state ratification conventions and by prominent individuals such as Thomas Jefferson (who was not a delegate to the Constitutional Convention). These critics argued that without further restraints, the strong central government would become tyrannical. The amendments were proposed by Congress as part of a block of twelve in September 1789. By December 1791 a sufficient number of states had ratified ten of the twelve proposals, and the Bill of Rights became part of the Constitution.

It is commonly understood that the Bill of Rights was not originally intended to apply to the states, though except where amendments refer specifically to the Federal Government or a branch thereof (as in the first amendment, under which some states in the early years of the nation officially established a religion), there is no such delineation in the text itself. Nevertheless, a general interpretation of inapplicability to the states remained until 1868, when the Fourteenth Amendment was passed, which stated, in part, that:

"No State shall make or enforce any law which shall abridge the privileges or immunities of citizens of the United States; nor shall any State deprive any person of life, liberty, or property, without due process of law; nor deny to any person within its jurisdiction the equal protection of the laws."

The Supreme Court has interpreted this clause to extend most, but not all, parts of the Bill of Rights to the states. Nevertheless, the balance of state and federal power has remained a battle in the Supreme Court.

The amendments that became the Bill of Rights were actually the last ten of the twelve amendments proposed in 1789. The second of the twelve proposed amendments, regarding the compensation of members of Congress, remained unratified until 1992, when the legislatures of enough states finally approved it and, as a result, it became the Twenty-seventh Amendment despite more than two centuries of pendency. The first of the twelve—still technically pending before the state legislatures for ratification—pertains to the apportionment of the United States House of Representatives after each decennial census. The most recent state whose lawmakers are known to have ratified this proposal is Kentucky in 1792, during that commonwealth's first month of statehood.

* First Amendment: addresses the rights of freedom of religion (prohibiting Congressional establishment of a religion over another religion through Law and protecting the right to free

exercise of religion), freedom of speech, freedom of the press, freedom of assembly, and freedom of petition.

* Second Amendment: declares "a well regulated militia" as "necessary to the security of a free State", and as explanation for prohibiting infringement of "the right of the People to keep and bear arms."

* Third Amendment: prohibits the government from using private homes as quarters for soldiers without the consent of the owners. The only existing case law regarding this amendment is a lower court decision in the case of Engblom v. Carey. [1]

* Fourth Amendment: guards against searches, arrests, and seizures of property without a specific warrant or a "probable cause" to believe a crime has been committed. Some rights to privacy have been inferred from this amendment and others by the Supreme Court.

* Fifth Amendment: forbids trial for a major crime except after indictment by a grand jury; prohibits

double jeopardy (repeated trials), except in certain very limited circumstances; forbids punishment without due process of law; and provides that an accused person may not be compelled to testify against himself (this is also known as "Taking the Fifth" or "Pleading the Fifth"). This is regarded as the "rights of the accused" amendment. It also prohibits government from taking private property without "just compensation," the basis of eminent domain in the United States.

* Sixth Amendment: guarantees a speedy public trial for criminal offenses. It requires trial by a jury, guarantees the right to legal counsel for the accused, and guarantees that the accused may require witnesses to attend the trial and testify in the presence of the accused. It also guarantees the accused a right to know the charges against him. The Sixth Amendment has several court cases associated with it, including Powell v. Alabama, United States v. Wong Kim Ark, Gideon v. Wainwright, and Crawford v. Washington. In 1966, the Supreme Court ruled that the fifth amendment prohibition on forced self-incrimination and the sixth amendment clause on right to counsel were to be made known to all

persons placed under arrest, and these clauses have become known as the Miranda rights.

* Seventh Amendment: assures trial by jury in civil cases.

* Eighth Amendment: forbids excessive bail or fines, and cruel and unusual punishment.

* Ninth Amendment: declares that the listing of individual rights in the Constitution and Bill of Rights is not meant to be comprehensive; and that the other rights not specifically mentioned are retained elsewhere by the people.

* Tenth Amendment: provides that powers that the Constitution does not delegate to the United States and does not prohibit the states from exercising, are "reserved to the States respectively, or to the people."

Subsequent Amendments (11–27)

Amendments to the Constitution subsequent to the Bill of Rights cover many subjects. The majority of the seventeen later amendments stem from continued efforts to expand individual civil or political liberties, while a few are concerned with modifying the basic governmental structure drafted in Philadelphia in 1787. Although the United States Constitution has been amended a total of 27 times, only 26 of the amendments are currently used because the 21st amendment supersedes the 18th.

* Eleventh Amendment (1795): Clarifies judicial power over foreign nationals, and limits ability of citizens to sue states in federal courts and under federal law.

* Twelfth Amendment (1804): Changes the method of presidential elections so that members of the electoral college cast separate ballots for president and vice president.

* Thirteenth Amendment (1865): Abolishes slavery and grants Congress power to enforce abolition.

* Fourteenth Amendment (1868): Defines United States citizenship; prohibits states from abridging citizens' privileges or immunities and rights to due

process and the equal protection of the law; repeals the Three-fifths compromise; prohibits repudiation of the federal debt caused by the Civil War.

* Fifteenth Amendment (1870): Forbids the federal government and the states from using a citizen's race, color, or previous status as a slave as a qualification for voting. (Full text)

* Sixteenth Amendment (1913): Authorizes unapportioned federal taxes on income. (Full text)

* Seventeenth Amendment (1913): Establishes direct election of senators.

* Eighteenth Amendment (1919): Prohibited the manufacturing, importing, and exporting of alcoholic beverages (see Prohibition in the United States). Repealed by the Twenty-First Amendment.

* Nineteenth Amendment (1920): Prohibits the federal government and the states from forbidding any citizen to vote due to their sex.

* Twentieth Amendment (1933): Changes details of Congressional and presidential terms and of presidential succession.

* Twenty-first Amendment (1933): Repeals Eighteenth Amendment. Permits states to prohibit the importation of alcoholic beverages.

* Twenty-second Amendment (1951): Limits president to two terms.

* Twenty-third Amendment (1961): Grants presidential electors to the District of Columbia.

* Twenty-fourth Amendment (1964): Prohibits the federal government and the states from requiring the payment of a tax as a qualification for voting for federal officials. (Full text)

* Twenty-fifth Amendment (1967): Changes details of presidential succession, provides for temporary removal of president, and provides for replacement of the vice president. (Full text)

* Twenty-sixth Amendment (1971): Prohibits the federal government and the states from forbidding

any citizen of age 18 or greater to vote simply because of their age.

* Twenty-seventh Amendment (1992): Limits congressional pay raises.

Unratified Amendments

Over 10,000 Constitutional amendments have been introduced in Congress since 1789; in a typical Congressional year in the last several decades, between 100 and 200 are offered. Most of these concepts never get out of Congressional committee, and far fewer get proposed by the Congress for ratification. Backers of some amendments have attempted the alternative, and thus-far never-utilized, method mentioned in Article Five. In two instances—reapportionment in the 1960s and a balanced federal budget during the 1970s and 1980s—these attempts have come within just two state legislative "applications" of triggering that alternative method.

Of the thirty-three amendments that have been proposed by Congress, six have failed ratification by the required three-quarters of the state legislatures—and four of those six are still technically pending before state lawmakers (see Coleman v. Miller). Starting with the 18th Amendment, each proposed amendment (except for the 19th Amendment and for the still-pending Child Labor Amendment of 1924) has specified a deadline for passage. The following are the unratified amendments:

* The Congressional Apportionment Amendment, proposed by the 1st Congress on September 25, 1789, defined a formula for how many members there would be in the United States House of Representatives after each decennial census. Ratified by eleven states, the last being Kentucky in June 1792 (Kentucky's initial month of statehood), this amendment contains no expiration date for ratification. In principle it may yet be ratified, though as written it became moot when the population of the United States reached ten million.

* The so-called the missing thirteenth amendment|missing thirteenth amendment, or "Titles of Nobility Amendment" (TONA), proposed by the 11th Congress on May 1, 1810,

would have ended the citizenship of any American accepting "any Title of Nobility or Honour" from any foreign power. Some maintain that the amendment was actually ratified by the legislatures of enough states, and that a conspiracy has suppressed it, but this has been thoroughly debunked [2]. Known to have been ratified by lawmakers in twelve states, the last in 1812, this amendment contains no expiration date for ratification. It may yet be ratified.

* The Corwin amendment, proposed by the 36th Congress on March 2, 1861, would have forbidden any attempt to subsequently amend the Constitution to empower the Federal government to "abolish or interfere" with the "domestic institutions" of the states (a delicate way of referring to slavery). It was ratified by only Ohio and Maryland lawmakers before the outbreak of the Civil War. Illinois lawmakers—sitting as a state constitutional convention at the time—likewise approved it, but that action is of questionable validity. The proposed amendment contains no expiration date for ratification and may yet be ratified. However, adoption of the 13th, 14th, and 15th Amendments after the Civil

War likely means that the amendment would be ineffective if adopted.

* A child labor amendment proposed by the 68th Congress on June 2, 1924, which stipulates: "The Congress shall have power to limit, regulate, and prohibit the labor of persons under eighteen years of age." This amendment is now moot, since subsequent federal child labor laws have uniformly been upheld as a valid exercise of Congress' powers under the commerce clause. This amendment contains no expiration date for ratification. It may yet be ratified.

Properly placed in a separate category from the other four constitutional amendments that Congress proposed to the states, but which not enough states have approved, are the following two offerings which—because of deadlines—are no longer subject to ratification.

* The Equal Rights Amendment, or ERA, which reads in pertinent part "Equality of rights under the law shall not be denied or abridged by the United States or by any state on account of sex." Proposed by the 92nd Congress on March 22,

1972, it was ratified by the legislatures of 35 states, and expired on either March 22, 1979 or on June 30, 1982, depending upon one's point of view of a controversial three-year extension of the ratification deadline, which was passed by the 95th Congress in 1978. Of the 35 states ratifying it, four later rescinded their ratifications prior to the extended ratification period which commenced March 23, 1979 and a fifth—while not going so far as to actually rescind its earlier ratification— adopted a resolution stipulating that its approval would not extend beyond March 22, 1979. There continues to be diversity of opinion as to whether such reversals are valid; no court has ruled on the question, including the Supreme Court. But a precedent against the validity of rescission was first established during the ratification process of the 14th Amendment when Ohio and New Jersey rescinded their earlier approvals, but yet were counted as ratifying states when the 14th Amendment was ultimately proclaimed part of the Constitution in 1868.

* The District of Columbia Voting Rights Amendment was proposed by the 95th Congress on August 22, 1978. Had it been ratified, it would

have granted to Washington, D.C. two Senators and at least one member of the House of Representatives as though the District of Columbia were a state. Ratified by the legislatures of only 16 states—less than half of the required 38—the proposed amendment expired on August 22, 1985.

There are currently only a few proposals for amendments which have entered mainstream political debate. These include the proposed Federal Marriage Amendment, the Balanced Budget Amendment, and the Flag Desecration Amendment.

For Know-It-Alls

Notes

1. WikiSource. WikiSource: Constitution of the United States of America. Retrieved on 2007-12-16.

2. Library of Congress. Primary Documents in American History: The United States Constitution. Retrieved on 2007-12-16.

3. Casey (1974)

4. Among possible exceptions is San Marino's Statutes of 1600, whose status as a true constitution is disputed by scholars.

5. NARA. Constitution of the United States — Questions and Answers. Retrieved on 2007-12-13.

6. NARA. National Archives Article on the Constitutional Convention. Retrieved on 2007-12-16.

7. NARA. National Archives Article on the Constitution. Retrieved on 2007-12-16.

8. NARA. National Archives Article on James Madison. Retrieved on 2007-12-16.

9. NARA. National Archives Article on the Entire Constitutional Convention. Retrieved on 2007-12-16.

10. NARA. National Archives Article on William Patterson. Retrieved on 2007-12-16.

11. NARA. National Archives Article on Roger Sherman. Retrieved on 2007-12-16.

12. NARA. National Archives Article on the Bill of Rights. Retrieved on 2007-12-16.

[edit] References

[edit] Primary sources

* Bailyn, Bernard, ed. The Debate on the Constitution: Federalist and Antifederalist Speeches, Articles, and Letters During the Struggle for Ratification. Part One: September

1787 to February 1788 (The Library of America, 1993) ISBN 0-940450-42-9

* Bailyn, Bernard, ed. The Debate on the Constitution: Federalist and Antifederalist Speeches, Articles, and Letters During the Struggle for Ratification. Part Two: January to August 1788 (The Library of America, 1993) ISBN 0-940450-64-X

* Garvey, John H. ed. Modern Constitutional Theory: A Reader 5th ed 2004; 820pp.

* Mason, Alpheus Thomas and Donald Grier Stephenson, ed. American Constitutional Law: Introductory Essays and Selected Cases (14th Edition) (2004)

* Tribe, Laurence H. American Constitutional Law (1999)

[edit] Reference books

* Hall, Kermit, ed. The Oxford Companion to the Supreme Court of the United States. Oxford U. Press, 1992. 1032 pp.

* Levy, Leonard W. et al., ed. Encyclopedia of the American Constitution. 5 vol; 1992; 3000 pp

* US Law Dictionary

Secondary Sources

* Amar, Akhil Reed (2005). "In the Beginning", America's Constitution: A Biography. New York: Random House. ISBN 1-4000-6262-4.

* Anastaplo, George, "Reflections on Constitutional Law" 2006 ISBN 0-8131-9156-4

* Beard, Charles. An Economic Interpretation of the Constitution of the United States, 1913.

* Richard R. Beeman, Stephen Botein, and Edward C., Carter, II, eds., Beyond Confederation: Origins of the Constitution and American National Identity (University of North Carolina Press, 1987);

* Gregory Casey. "The Supreme Court and Myth: An Empirical Investigation," Law & Society Review, Vol. 8, No. 3 (Spring, 1974), pp. 385–420

* Countryman, Edward, ed. What Did the Constitution Mean to Early Americans.Bedford/St.

Martin's, 1999. xii + 169 pp. online review ISBN 0-312-18262-7.

* Edling, Max M. (2003). A Revolution in Favor of Government: Origins of the U.S. Constitution and the Making of the American State. Oxford University Press. ISBN 0-19-514870-3.

* Ely, James W., Jr. The Guardian of Every Other Right: A Constitutional History of Property Rights. Oxford U. Press, 1992. 193 pp.

* Fallon, Richard H. (2004). The Dynamic Constitution: An Introduction to American Constitutional Law. Cambridge University Press. ISBN 0-521-84094-5.

* Finkelman, Paul. Slavery and the Founders: Race and Slavery in the Age of Jefferson (M.E. Sharpe, 1996);

* Hoffer, Peter Charles. The Law's Conscience: Equitable Constitutionalism in America. U. of North Carolina Press, 1990. 301 pp.

* Irons, Peter. A People's History of the Supreme Court. 2000. 542 pp.

* Kammen, Michael (1986). A Machine that Would Go of Itself: The Constitution in American Culture. New York: Alfred A. Knopf. ISBN 0-394-52905-7.

* Kelly, Alfred Hinsey; Harbison, Winfred Audif; Belz, Herman (1991). The American Constitution: its origins and development, 7th edition, New York: Norton & Co. ISBN 0-393-96119-2.

* Kersch, Ken I. Constructing Civil Liberties: Discontinuities in the Development of American Constitutional Law. Cambridge U. Press, 2004. 392 pp.

* Kyvig, David E. Explicit and Authentic Acts: Amending the U.S. Constitution, 1776–1995. U. Press of Kansas, 1996. 604 pp.

* Levin, Daniel Lessard. Representing Popular Sovereignty: The Constitution in American Political Culture. State U. of New York Press., 1999. 283 pp.

* Licht, Robert A., ed. The Framers and Fundamental Rights. American Enterprise Inst. Press, 1991. 194 pp.

* Marshall, Thurgood, "The Constitution: A Living Document," Howard Law Journal 1987: 623-28.

* Powell, H. Jefferson. A Community Built on Words: The Constitution in History and Politics. U. of Chicago Press, 2002. 251 pp.

* Rakove, Jack N. Original Meanings: Politics and Ideas in the Making of the Constitution. Knopf, 1996. 455 pp.

* Sandoz, Ellis. A Government of Laws: Political Theory, Religion, and the American Founding. Louisiana State U. Press, 1990. 259 pp.

* Sheldon, Charles H. Essentials of Constitutional Law: The Supreme Court and the Fundamental Law (2001) 208 pp

* VanBurkleo, Sandra F.; Hall, Kermit L.; and Kaczorowski, Robert J., eds. Constitutionalism and American Culture: Writing the New Constitutional History. U. Press of Kansas, 2002. 464 pp.

* Mazzone, Jason (2005). "The Creation of a Constitutional Culture". Tulsa Law Review 40: 671.

* Smith, Jean Edward; Levine, Herbert M. (1988). Civil Liberties & Civil Rights Debated. Englewood Cliffs, New Jersey: Prentice Hall.

* Smith, Jean Edward (1989). The Constitution and American Foreign Policy. St. Paul, MN: West Publishing Company.

* Black, G. Edward. The Constitution and the New Deal. Harvard U. Press, 2000. 385 pp.

* Wiecek, William M., "The Witch at the Christening: Slavery and the Constitution's Origins," Leonard W. Levy and Dennis J. Mahoney, eds., The Framing and Ratification of the Constitution (Macmillan, 1987), 178-84.

For Know-It-Alls

Further Reading

* Klos, Stanley L. (2004). President Who? Forgotten Founders. Pittsburgh, Pennsylvania: Evisum, Inc., 261. ISBN 0-9752627-5-0.

For Know-It-Alls

GNU Free Documentation License

Version 1.2, November 2002

0. PREAMBLE

The purpose of this License is to make a manual, textbook, or other
functional and useful document "free" in the sense of freedom: to assure
everyone the effective freedom to copy and redistribute it, with or without
modifying it, either commercially or noncommercially. Secondarily, this
License preserves for the author and publisher a way to get credit for their
work, while not being considered responsible for modifications made by
others.

This License is a kind of "copyleft", which means that derivative works of
the document must themselves be free in the same sense. It complements
the GNU General Public License, which is a copyleft license designed for
free software.

We have designed this License in order to use it for manuals for free
software, because free software needs free documentation: a free program
should come with manuals providing the same freedoms that the software
does. But this License is not limited to software manuals; it can be used for
any textual work, regardless of subject matter or whether it is published as a
printed book. We recommend this License principally for works whose
purpose is instruction or reference.

1. APPLICABILITY AND DEFINITIONS

This License applies to any manual or other work, in any medium, that contains a notice placed by the copyright holder saying it can be distributed under the terms of this License. Such a notice grants a world-wide, royalty-free license, unlimited in duration, to use that work under the conditions stated herein. The "Document", below, refers to any such manual or work. Any member of the public is a licensee, and is addressed as "you". You accept the license if you copy, modify or distribute the work in a way requiring permission under copyright law.

A "Modified Version" of the Document means any work containing the Document or a portion of it, either copied verbatim, or with modifications and/or translated into another language.

A "Secondary Section" is a named appendix or a front-matter section of the Document that deals exclusively with the relationship of the publishers or authors of the Document to the Document's overall subject (or to related matters) and contains nothing that could fall directly within that overall subject. (Thus, if the Document is in part a textbook of mathematics, a Secondary Section may not explain any mathematics.) The relationship could be a matter of historical connection with the subject or with related matters, or of legal, commercial, philosophical, ethical or political position regarding them.

The "Invariant Sections" are certain Secondary Sections whose titles are designated, as being those of Invariant Sections, in the notice that says that the Document is released under this License. If a section does not fit the above definition of Secondary then it is not allowed to be designated as Invariant. The Document may contain zero Invariant Sections. If the Document does not identify any Invariant Sections then there are none.

The "Cover Texts" are certain short passages of text that are listed, as Front-Cover Texts or Back-Cover Texts, in the notice that says that the Document is released under this License. A Front-Cover Text may be at most 5 words, and a Back-Cover Text may be at most 25 words.

The United States Constitution

A "Transparent" copy of the Document means a machine-readable copy, represented in a format whose specification is available to the general public, that is suitable for revising the document straightforwardly with generic text editors or (for images composed of pixels) generic paint programs or (for drawings) some widely available drawing editor, and that is suitable for input to text formatters or for automatic translation to a variety of formats suitable for input to text formatters. A copy made in an otherwise Transparent file format whose markup, or absence of markup, has been arranged to thwart or discourage subsequent modification by readers is not Transparent. An image format is not Transparent if used for any substantial amount of text. A copy that is not "Transparent" is called "Opaque".

Examples of suitable formats for Transparent copies include plain ASCII without markup, Texinfo input format, LaTeX input format, SGML or XML using a publicly available DTD, and standard-conforming simple HTML, PostScript or PDF designed for human modification. Examples of transparent image formats include PNG, XCF and JPG. Opaque formats include proprietary formats that can be read and edited only by proprietary word processors, SGML or XML for which the DTD and/or processing tools are not generally available, and the machine-generated HTML, PostScript or PDF produced by some word processors for output purposes only.

The "Title Page" means, for a printed book, the title page itself, plus such following pages as are needed to hold, legibly, the material this License requires to appear in the title page. For works in formats which do not have any title page as such, "Title Page" means the text near the most prominent appearance of the work's title, preceding the beginning of the body of the text.

A section "Entitled XYZ" means a named subunit of the Document whose title either is precisely XYZ or contains XYZ in parentheses following text that translates XYZ in another language. (Here XYZ stands for a specific section name mentioned below, such as "Acknowledgements", "Dedications", "Endorsements", or "History".) To "Preserve the Title" of such a section when you modify the Document means that it remains a section "Entitled XYZ" according to this definition.

For Know-It-Alls

The Document may include Warranty Disclaimers next to the notice which states that this License applies to the Document. These Warranty Disclaimers are considered to be included by reference in this License, but only as regards disclaiming warranties: any other implication that these Warranty Disclaimers may have is void and has no effect on the meaning of this License.

2. VERBATIM COPYING

You may copy and distribute the Document in any medium, either commercially or noncommercially, provided that this License, the copyright notices, and the license notice saying this License applies to the Document are reproduced in all copies, and that you add no other conditions whatsoever to those of this License. You may not use technical measures to obstruct or control the reading or further copying of the copies you make or distribute. However, you may accept compensation in exchange for copies. If you distribute a large enough number of copies you must also follow the conditions in section 3.

You may also lend copies, under the same conditions stated above, and you may publicly display copies.

3. COPYING IN QUANTITY

If you publish printed copies (or copies in media that commonly have printed covers) of the Document, numbering more than 100, and the Document's license notice requires Cover Texts, you must enclose the copies in covers that carry, clearly and legibly, all these Cover Texts: Front-Cover Texts on the front cover, and Back-Cover Texts on the back cover. Both covers must also clearly and legibly identify you as the publisher of these copies. The front cover must present the full title with all words of the title equally prominent and visible. You may add other material on the covers in addition. Copying with changes limited to the covers, as long as they preserve the title of the Document and satisfy these conditions, can be treated as verbatim copying in other respects.

If the required texts for either cover are too voluminous to fit legibly, you should put the first ones listed (as many as fit reasonably) on the actual cover, and continue the rest onto adjacent pages.

If you publish or distribute Opaque copies of the Document numbering more than 100, you must either include a machine-readable Transparent copy along with each Opaque copy, or state in or with each Opaque copy a computer-network location from which the general network-using public has access to download using public-standard network protocols a complete Transparent copy of the Document, free of added material. If you use the latter option, you must take reasonably prudent steps, when you begin distribution of Opaque copies in quantity, to ensure that this Transparent copy will remain thus accessible at the stated location until at least one year after the last time you distribute an Opaque copy (directly or through your agents or retailers) of that edition to the public.

It is requested, but not required, that you contact the authors of the Document well before redistributing any large number of copies, to give them a chance to provide you with an updated version of the Document.

4. MODIFICATIONS

You may copy and distribute a Modified Version of the Document under the conditions of sections 2 and 3 above, provided that you release the Modified Version under precisely this License, with the Modified Version filling the role of the Document, thus licensing distribution and modification of the Modified Version to whoever possesses a copy of it. In addition, you must do these things in the Modified Version:

 * A. Use in the Title Page (and on the covers, if any) a title distinct from that of the Document, and from those of previous versions (which should, if there were any, be listed in the History section of the Document). You may use the same title as a previous version if the original publisher of that version gives permission.
 * B. List on the Title Page, as authors, one or more persons or entities responsible for authorship of the modifications in the Modified Version, together with at least five of the principal authors of the Document (all of its principal authors, if it has fewer than five), unless they release you from this requirement.
 * C. State on the Title page the name of the publisher of the Modified Version, as the publisher.
 * D. Preserve all the copyright notices of the Document.

* E. Add an appropriate copyright notice for your modifications adjacent to the other copyright notices.

* F. Include, immediately after the copyright notices, a license notice giving the public permission to use the Modified Version under the terms of this License, in the form shown in the Addendum below.

* G. Preserve in that license notice the full lists of Invariant Sections and required Cover Texts given in the Document's license notice.

* H. Include an unaltered copy of this License.

* I. Preserve the section Entitled "History", Preserve its Title, and add to it an item stating at least the title, year, new authors, and publisher of the Modified Version as given on the Title Page. If there is no section Entitled "History" in the Document, create one stating the title, year, authors, and publisher of the Document as given on its Title Page, then add an item describing the Modified Version as stated in the previous sentence.

* J. Preserve the network location, if any, given in the Document for public access to a Transparent copy of the Document, and likewise the network locations given in the Document for previous versions it was based on. These may be placed in the "History" section. You may omit a network location for a work that was published at least four years before the Document itself, or if the original publisher of the version it refers to gives permission.

* K. For any section Entitled "Acknowledgements" or "Dedications", Preserve the Title of the section, and preserve in the section all the substance and tone of each of the contributor acknowledgements and/or dedications given therein.

* L. Preserve all the Invariant Sections of the Document, unaltered in their text and in their titles. Section numbers or the equivalent are not considered part of the section titles.

* M. Delete any section Entitled "Endorsements". Such a section may not be included in the Modified Version.

* N. Do not retitle any existing section to be Entitled "Endorsements" or to conflict in title with any Invariant Section.

* O. Preserve any Warranty Disclaimers.

If the Modified Version includes new front-matter sections or appendices that qualify as Secondary Sections and contain no material copied from the Document, you may at your option designate some or all of these sections as invariant. To do this, add their titles to the list of Invariant Sections in the

Modified Version's license notice. These titles must be distinct from any other section titles.

You may add a section Entitled "Endorsements", provided it contains nothing but endorsements of your Modified Version by various parties--for example, statements of peer review or that the text has been approved by an organization as the authoritative definition of a standard.

You may add a passage of up to five words as a Front-Cover Text, and a passage of up to 25 words as a Back-Cover Text, to the end of the list of Cover Texts in the Modified Version. Only one passage of Front-Cover Text and one of Back-Cover Text may be added by (or through arrangements made by) any one entity. If the Document already includes a cover text for the same cover, previously added by you or by arrangement made by the same entity you are acting on behalf of, you may not add another; but you may replace the old one, on explicit permission from the previous publisher that added the old one.

The author(s) and publisher(s) of the Document do not by this License give permission to use their names for publicity for or to assert or imply endorsement of any Modified Version.

5. COMBINING DOCUMENTS

You may combine the Document with other documents released under this License, under the terms defined in section 4 above for modified versions, provided that you include in the combination all of the Invariant Sections of all of the original documents, unmodified, and list them all as Invariant Sections of your combined work in its license notice, and that you preserve all their Warranty Disclaimers.

The combined work need only contain one copy of this License, and multiple identical Invariant Sections may be replaced with a single copy. If there are multiple Invariant Sections with the same name but different contents, make the title of each such section unique by adding at the end of it, in parentheses, the name of the original author or publisher of that section if known, or else a unique number. Make the same adjustment to the section titles in the list of Invariant Sections in the license notice of the combined work.

In the combination, you must combine any sections Entitled "History" in the various original documents, forming one section Entitled "History"; likewise combine any sections Entitled "Acknowledgements", and any sections Entitled "Dedications". You must delete all sections Entitled "Endorsements."

6. COLLECTIONS OF DOCUMENTS

You may make a collection consisting of the Document and other documents released under this License, and replace the individual copies of this License in the various documents with a single copy that is included in the collection, provided that you follow the rules of this License for verbatim copying of each of the documents in all other respects.

You may extract a single document from such a collection, and distribute it individually under this License, provided you insert a copy of this License into the extracted document, and follow this License in all other respects regarding verbatim copying of that document.

7. AGGREGATION WITH INDEPENDENT WORKS

A compilation of the Document or its derivatives with other separate and independent documents or works, in or on a volume of a storage or distribution medium, is called an "aggregate" if the copyright resulting from the compilation is not used to limit the legal rights of the compilation's users beyond what the individual works permit. When the Document is included in an aggregate, this License does not apply to the other works in the aggregate which are not themselves derivative works of the Document.

If the Cover Text requirement of section 3 is applicable to these copies of the Document, then if the Document is less than one half of the entire aggregate, the Document's Cover Texts may be placed on covers that bracket the Document within the aggregate, or the electronic equivalent of covers if the Document is in electronic form. Otherwise they must appear on printed covers that bracket the whole aggregate.

8. TRANSLATION

Translation is considered a kind of modification, so you may distribute translations of the Document under the terms of section 4. Replacing Invariant Sections with translations requires special permission from their copyright holders, but you may include translations of some or all Invariant Sections in addition to the original versions of these Invariant Sections. You may include a translation of this License, and all the license notices in the Document, and any Warranty Disclaimers, provided that you also include the original English version of this License and the original versions of those notices and disclaimers. In case of a disagreement between the translation and the original version of this License or a notice or disclaimer, the original version will prevail.

If a section in the Document is Entitled "Acknowledgements", "Dedications", or "History", the requirement (section 4) to Preserve its Title (section 1) will typically require changing the actual title.

9. TERMINATION

You may not copy, modify, sublicense, or distribute the Document except as expressly provided for under this License. Any other attempt to copy, modify, sublicense or distribute the Document is void, and will automatically terminate your rights under this License. However, parties who have received copies, or rights, from you under this License will not have their licenses terminated so long as such parties remain in full compliance.

10. FUTURE REVISIONS OF THIS LICENSE

The Free Software Foundation may publish new, revised versions of the GNU Free Documentation License from time to time. Such new versions will be similar in spirit to the present version, but may differ in detail to address new problems or concerns. See http://www.gnu.org/copyleft/.

Each version of the License is given a distinguishing version number. If the Document specifies that a particular numbered version of this License "or any later version" applies to it, you have the option of following the terms and conditions either of that specified version or of any later version that has been published (not as a draft) by the Free Software Foundation. If the Document does not specify a version number of this License, you may choose any version ever published (not as a draft) by the Free Software Foundation.

How to use this License for your documents

To use this License in a document you have written, include a copy of the License in the document and put the following copyright and license notices just after the title page:

Copyright (c) YEAR YOUR NAME.
Permission is granted to copy, distribute and/or modify this document under the terms of the GNU Free Documentation License, Version 1.2 or any later version published by the Free Software Foundation; with no Invariant Sections, no Front-Cover Texts, and no Back-Cover Texts. A copy of the license is included in the section entitled "GNU
Free Documentation License".

If you have Invariant Sections, Front-Cover Texts and Back-Cover Texts, replace the "with...Texts." line with this:

with the Invariant Sections being LIST THEIR TITLES, with the Front-Cover Texts being LIST, and with the Back-Cover Texts being LIST.

If you have Invariant Sections without Cover Texts, or some other combination of the three, merge those two alternatives to suit the situation.

If your document contains nontrivial examples of program code, we recommend releasing these examples in parallel under your choice of free software license, such as the GNU General Public License, to permit their use in free software.

Printed in the United States
134356LV00005B/125/P

9 781599 862248